STROKE
OF
MY HEART

Healing after the Battle Within

Hyvelle Ferguson-Davis

Dedication

This book is dedicated to my heavenly father and everyone He has allowed in my life, my family, friends, and those struggling to find balance despite a diagnosis or prognosis.

CONTENTS

INTRODUCTION: Lifting the Veil 7

CHAPTER 01: My Abandoned Heart 9

CHAPTER 02: A Heart Betrayed 15

CHAPTER 03: The Root of My Heart 21

CHAPTER 04: Up Against the World 27

CHAPTER 05: A Warning Signal 33

CHAPTER 06: Masking the Pain 41

CHAPTER 07: The Unknown 45

CHAPTER 08: Loss of Identity 53

CHAPTER 09: All Options Are Exhausted. 57

CHAPTER 10: The Unveiling 65

CHAPTER 11: A Moment of Reflection 71

CHAPTER 12: Monitor Your Health 73

CHAPTER 13: Reflections of Grace 89

Acknowledgments 93

Appendix 95

About the Author. 98

INTRODUCTION:
Lifting the Veil

Dealing with an illness or grappling with a shattered spirit poses immense challenges, hindering our ability to care for ourselves and our loved ones. We may try to control every aspect of life as we face these challenges, but finding balance remains pivotal. It is the anchor that allows us to thrive in a constantly changing world, especially when adversity requires us to be adaptable and innovative to sustain ourselves and those we cherish.

Inner strength, often hidden beneath layers of self-doubt and past trauma, reveals itself when all options are exhausted. For so many years, my strength lay dormant due to the weight of my preconceptions and the abuse I suffered. My burdens eventually manifested into illnesses, culminating in a sequence of events that crippled my body, causing vital organs to shut down. I suffered a stroke and a heart attack, which ultimately led to my undergoing an emergency quadruple open-heart bypass surgery. But I survived. I am a warrior and conqueror. My survival is a testament to grace.

The essence of a fulfilling life rests in the delicate balance between our spiritual, mental, and physical well-being. While each journey remains uniquely ours, our human connection thrives on faith and resilience. Trusting in God's supernatural abilities and surrendering to His plan is crucial to living out our divine purpose. Without this faith, stagnation looms large, rendering our lives void of fulfillment.

Faith in God does not mean everything will always be perfect. Obstacles, challenges, and hard times will persist, but faith emboldens us to keep going, searching for answers, and continuing to do whatever it takes to succeed. It's about developing an unbreakable belief that God could intervene and make His presence felt in our lives.

In those sleepless moments, when rest eludes us and we are consumed with trying to control situations that are out of our hands, what shows up is our innate instinct as women to shoulder the burden of resolving life's complexities. Rooted in our very existence since the Garden of Eden, where God planted feelings of enmity within us, this impulse fuels our roles as caregivers, problem solvers, and pillars of support. Yet, amidst this endless giving, we must pause, assess our lives, and find our balance. It's time to take a moment to reflect on how we're truly living, or perhaps merely surviving.

CHAPTER 1
MY ABANDONED HEART

My life was full of heartache. The people that should have protected my innocence failed miserably. It was as if I was thrown out as a wounded animal to a pack of wolves. In some ways, this lost, frail 8-year-old little girl is still trapped inside me. She longs to feel that love, protection, and security every child deserves. And because of that, I'm still waiting for my parents to rescue me. Now that I am grown, I have discovered that my trust issues stem from my past. Consequently, I lived a guarded life and carried around enormous guilt. These experiences robbed me of my identity.

Have you ever been in a place trapped in utter darkness or felt a heavy sense of loneliness closing in on you like an ominous storm cloud? I felt this way as if my entire world was shattered into a million pieces. I knew that there was no way that I could ever put all the scattered pieces of my life back together. And because I never dealt with the pain from my childhood, it finally caught up with me.

The invisible veil I had worn to protect myself from emotional harm had left me broken, without an understanding of what a genuine, meaningful relationship should be. I know now that what I used to protect myself only alienated me from experiencing real growth and development. Due to my suppressed emotions,

I lived an isolated life and felt horrified when I was touched by others. The dual sense of wanting and not wanting to feel was so hard to accept that it furthered my anguish. For a long time, I just went through the motions.

I had built a cocoon around myself that made me feel unsure of everything. I acted out and started expressing myself with unhealthy behaviors as a means of an outlet. I thought that I would never be good enough for anything or anyone. I was always in survival mode. I lacked empathy, which caused me to sabotage many potentially meaningful relationships. I always kept people at bay, never wanting to get close to anyone.

I attributed my feelings of insecurities and unworthiness to not being genuinely accepted by my father. It all began when my father met my mother in 1959. My father was much older than my mother, thirty-two years her senior. His oldest son is older than my mother! My father was a sailor who owned ships that sailed the Caribbean seas. On one of his many voyages, he made a refueling stop on the beautiful island of Haiti. Haiti was the poorest country in the Western Hemisphere, but rich in culture and filled with bountiful natural resources such as salt, sugar, and wood. I'm not sure of the sequence of the story or how it unfolded, but I heard that my father was promised my mother's eldest sister as a bride. He was considered to be well off back in those days. When he saw my mother on a visit to the home, he desired her instead. She was young and beautiful. And at the tender age of fourteen, my mother was given to my father for a price. I was told by my mother that back in those days in Haiti if someone wanted a wife, he had to pay a dowry to the bride's father, and that person would also take care of the bride's family, which was exactly what my father did.

My mother was shipped off to the Bahamas after marrying a man she barely knew, a land she did not know. Just like Miss Sealy from "The Color Purple," my mother suffered an unspoken life of pain and misery from my father. She dealt with absence, infidelity, emotional abuse, and physical abuse–not to mention the abuse my siblings told me about their interactions with my father. There are even stories of my mother having to take care of children my father brought home from another relationship.

I had so many questions that I wanted to ask my mother about her life, but I knew that doing so would bring about so many painful memories. I would see the anguish in her eyes just by the mere mention of my father's name or any situation relating to him because she still had nightmares. I finally realized that I had to stop questioning her about him. Still, I thought he could not have been all that terrible. I wanted to know what kind of person he was and about his past, if he knew how to love, and why did he leave. Alas, I knew that my questions would never be answered because I could not continue to see the pain that it caused my mother every time I mentioned his name. I wondered if my father was capable of loving anyone. Not knowing the answers to my questions left a void within me.

I was the sixth of my mother's twelve children; two died at birth. I always thought that she never wanted any children because she detested my father. I was four when my father left, at that time my mother was in her early thirties and seven months pregnant. I'm not entirely sure how the events unfolded. I believe that she finally had enough of the torment and kicked him out. Because he had always gone out to sea, my mother learned how to navigate her life and care for us without my father. So she kicked him out, and he never looked back, leaving my mother with just the house and no money to support us. My mother never worked a job when she and my father were together.

My siblings and I were devastated when he left, although he was not always physically present. We would be excited for the days he would come home with gifts for us from his travels. But, now we knew that we would not see him again.

I sometimes try to imagine how afraid or fearful my mom felt in those moments of being in a foreign land with ten small children, ranging from ages two to thirteen, with no family or income. At times, the kindness of neighbors and friends was our only means of support.

My mother surviving those years of hardship strengthened her resolve and made her adaptable to her circumstances. I was once told a story by my sister about how my mother started her business. She said one day my mother went to our cupboard and noticed only two cans of milk left. She knew that it was not enough to feed us, so she took one can to the neighbors to see if they wanted to buy it. The neighbor wanted them and paid three times the original price. With the money, my mother was able to buy more milk, igniting her spirit of entrepreneurship. She started selling evaporated milk and other items out of our pantry to the neighbors, eventually outfitting a small store in our house.

Women in our community had husbands and rarely had jobs that required them to work full-time. I watched my mother go from a housewife with no vocational skills to a full-time entrepreneur doing everything she could do without any formal training. Eventually, she bought a bus, became a bus driver, and was able to branch out.

To this day, I cannot remember my father's face, although I saw a black-and-white picture of him years ago. I longed to know if I had his smile, to see the color of his eyes, or to feel a hug of his big stature. How could you miss something that you never had? Yet, I still longed for his love and affection. I was always reminded of his absence. When I went to church and other events or even watched TV, I would imagine he would be with me. I had wished that Michael Landon from the TV show "Little House on the Prairie" was my father. This made me sad because I knew that he was never coming back to us. It consumed my thoughts. Even when I ventured across the street to play with my cousins, seeing their father coming home from work was a constant reminder that I did not have my own. It was like peeling a bandage off a new wound with every interaction. My mother once told me that I was his favorite child. It made no difference to me because as the year waned, I thought of him as no more than a sperm donor.

At one point, my mother started a clothing business while still driving the bus. This added an extra burden of not having her around the house. Then there were times my mother had to travel out of the country to buy merchandise to sell. With my mother gone so often, my oldest sister took on the role of caring for us. She was in her teens and did her best to handle the many responsibilities that fell to her. I admired my sister and disliked her at the same time. She always put our needs ahead of hers, but she was extremely vocal and had an authoritative approach to making sure we did our chores. She was a loving and fearless person, but also forceful. I was devastated when she moved to Miami to live with relatives. She wanted to get away to figure out what she wanted out of life. The only thing was that our biggest supporter was now gone. I felt abandoned once again.

"A violated heart where love has turned to disdain, promises lie broken, and trust has been irreparably damaged."

CHAPTER 2

A HEART BETRAYED

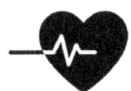

The family dynamics changed immediately after my oldest sister left the house. Everything became chaotic. She was the glue that held everything together, from feeding us early in the morning to making sure that we went to bed at night. I still had four older teenage brothers and two sisters–one was three years older and the other, two years younger than me. In a sense, my brothers were there, but they were all still young, trying to figure out their own lives.

My mother made countless sacrifices for our family. She worked tirelessly to take care of us, while also juggling being a woman, a mother, and multiple business ventures. Her days were filled with tasks from dawn till dusk–making breakfast before the sun rose, cleaning, doing laundry by hand, and even slaughtering live chickens for our meals. On Saturdays, we would all pitch in to help wash clothes outside and hang them to dry. Sundays were just as hectic, with my mother waking up early to cook a delicious dinner before getting us ready for church. She always made sure our hair was clean and presentable before rushing out the door. My mother's hard work and dedication never went unnoticed or unappreciated.

My mother met a younger, handsome man who drove one of her buses. He was tall and had light skin with light brown eyes. Initially, I didn't mind that he was around all the time. He was genuinely nice to us, always buying us goodies such as ice cream and toys. He would even take us for outings to the movies and to the beach, which was fun. He moved in and quickly became our stepfather.

Around seven or eight years old, life, once again, changed. It all started innocently enough, but things grew worse over time. I started noticing how impatient and forceful he was. If he wanted something done, we would have to stop what we were doing and quickly handle the task because he would beat us with his belt. We were not happy about his methods of discipline because we were not used to them. He was overwhelmed with the number of children in the house and all his new responsibilities. I was afraid of him at first, so I mostly kept out of his way.

My mother became pregnant again and our home, which was already bursting at the seams, was growing even bigger. We lived in a house with only one bathroom. Fortunately, we had running water, though some of our neighbors did not. I was always grateful for that because we did not have to draw water in buckets, so that made our lives much easier. Mom still ran her business while she was pregnant and kept us fed. Although she had a man living with us, she still was the breadwinner. In the early eighties, my mom traveled to many different countries. Back then, women rarely ventured off of our small island. Every time an opportunity presented itself, she grabbed hold of it.

As the months passed, she decided that she wanted to have her baby in the United States. Typically, if she needed to leave, it was only for a week or two. This time it was for an extended period.

In her absence, our stepfather became our sole caretaker, making sure we had what we needed. Weeks later, mom came back with a beautiful baby girl, and we were all excited. My baby sister was our Christmas present that year; she was born on December 24th. She brought so much joy to the household.

We were a family, and it felt good. We had a father who loved us–albeit stern in his approach–which I had never experienced. A father who would come home daily from work and give us treats was a beautiful thing. Mom did not have to work as much. Our stepdad was there to protect and take care of us, as a father would. Now, we were like other families around the neighborhood. In the following months, my mom was once again pregnant, and we were all happy about it because my mom was finally happy.

Our stepdad always paid close attention to me and made sure I took baths. He would say that I was his favorite, which made me feel special. I loved the feeling of having someone always around who was good to me. He was the father I always wanted, who showered me with adoration. Sometimes I would wait with excitement in anticipation for what he brought home for me that day–a soda, candy, or even money would make my day.

I was considered the prettiest of my sisters, and my mom made me feel that I was. She was so excited when my teacher suggested I enter the school's beauty pageant. I was so excited you could not tell me that I was not Cinderella. I was thin for my age, with long hair. My family called me Thread because I was so skinny.

I was also enrolled in ballet class, and my stepdad took me to and from classes. I loved it because he would give me a special treat every time. It was extremely satisfying to have someone look out for me like no one else.

Eventually, our rides home became longer. At first, it was innocent. He would ask, "Do you have a kiss for me today?" as he squeezed me even tighter. I loved the feeling. However, it got uncomfortable, and I was unsure how to react, how to feel, what to do, or what to say. I became terrified. An intentional touch that felt too long or a touch of my thighs that felt uncomfortable. Then he would ask, "What do you have for me today? Is there anything you want me to do? Do you love me?" I was confused. Of course, I loved him so I did what I could to please him.

I remember this one day he picked me up early from school on his bus. This ride stood out because we were driving for a long time when we did not live far from my school. Eventually, we arrived at a secluded beach. We were the only people there. I was a bit puzzled because it was in the middle of the day. He asked me if I wanted to go for a swim. I said, "No! I couldn't because I had on my school uniform." He told me to take off my skirt and swim in my underwear because we were the only people at the beach and no one could see us. I loved to swim and went along with it. He lifted me and carried me on his shoulder, carrying me into the water. It was fun as we swam and played games. Afterward, we ate and drank soda. It was one of the best days I've ever had. He told me not to tell anyone about our trip, and that was fine with me because I really felt special that day.

On another occasion, I remember my stepdad came to my school to pick me up early with my baby sister. I was so excited because I thought that we were going to the beach again, but he brought me home. No one was home, which was extremely uncommon because our house was always busy and full of people. It was just me, him, and my baby sister. Again, I thought we were going to the beach on our special trip, only to stop at home to get some clothes for the water. So I was excited. But this time, he acted a bit differently. He put my baby sister on the floor in her rocker and then walked over to me and picked me up. He carried me to a chair and sat me on his lap as he proceeded to kiss me. To this day, I only remember bits and pieces of what took place that day. I felt as if the brutality was happening to someone else and not me. And I'm still traumatized.

I have these flashes of blurred images of me lying on the brown carpet, eyes shut, and writhing in excruciating pain. My baby sister was crying. I was frightened as the blood drained down from my body and into the tub while he stood over me. Endless tears flowed down my face. I never looked into his eyes after that day. The abuse went on for years. I did not know how to react or how to get help. I wished that my real father would come and save me, but he never came, so I became angry and withdrawn from the world. I completely shut down.

Since that day, I do not remember much of my childhood. My mother did not consider that there was a lot of evil in this world, that evil came in the form of my stepfather, the animal that devoured my innocence. I went from a little girl desperately wanting her father's love, security, and protection to praying nightly for him to rescue me from my abuser.

I felt trapped, lonely, and desperate, but I also felt kind of special. Those feelings brought on a sense of guilt and shame. At first, I was confused and angry and then I learned to accept the situation. It reminds me of a dog that's being abused but still goes to its owner and shows genuine affection because that's all the dog knows. How can you love someone and fear them at the same time? I was an emotional wreck.

My stepfather moved out of our home some years later. I do not know what happened between him and my mom. My guess is that he found a younger woman with daughters whose innocence he could snatch. I did not care that he moved out. I never allowed myself to get wrapped up in those feelings. My mind was made up. I was going to expect the worst from everyone.

CHAPTER 3

THE ROOT OF MY HEART

After my stepfather left, I was void of feelings. I went to church and school pretending that I was fine. I was not. Because I was unable to trust my emotions or anyone else's motives, I became withdrawn. I had always felt like my voice was never heard coming from a home filled with a lot of people. I learned how to not be seen or heard. As an outlet, I became promiscuous with boys in my neighborhood. I knew the feeling. When a boy showed me affection and treated me nicely, I considered that a green light to reciprocate. It made me feel alive. A sense of sick gratitude, a terrible behavior I learned from my stepfather.

My behavior grew more troublesome as I became older. I would sneak out of our home for hours on end which became an issue for my mother. When she had finally had enough of me and would not tolerate my antics anymore, she sent me to live with my sister in Miami. I was almost fourteen at the time and clearly out of control. I was numb inside.

I was upset and angry about my move to Miami, and I barely spoke to my mom for months after she put me on a plane by myself.

I believed my mom meant well, but soon things went horribly wrong. I went from a school with 400 students to a school with over 3,000 students. I was a small fish swimming in an ocean with no help and no sense of direction. At first, I felt like a wallflower in high school and put little effort into schoolwork. Eventually, I began to navigate my way. The most impactful lesson I learned early on was to not take anyone's crap. Yep, I hardened myself even more. I no longer held anything in but reverted to the same old behaviors of acting out and seeking affection. The only difference was that I took control. Still, sadly, I continued to be very promiscuous with men. I thought that if I took more control of my so-called relationships, they would not disappoint me. The only thing is that that mindset closed me off from my feelings completely.

Nevertheless, my high school years were tolerable. I made the most of it despite my mom moving to Florida and wanting me to live with her. This move would have required me to leave the basketball team at school which I did not want to do. Still, I was not spending much time at my sister's house, always busy with school activities or sleepovers at my friend's house, where I would meet with whomever. I dated many men and even had relationships with older married men. I felt like older men understood me better, and I was okay with engaging with them sexually, although I was not mentally able to deal with the emotional attachments. I felt dirty and unworthy, so I shut down and carried on.

My last year of high school was fantastic; in addition to being on the basketball team, I also started playing volleyball where I developed a few genuine girl friendships with my teammates. This made me happy because we talked a lot about everything. They were so open and warm. I did not feel judged although our conversations were relatively light. We would talk about who we had a crush on, the boys on the baseball team, and the fact that we all had a schoolgirl crush on the rapper LL Cool J. Those days were the happiest times of my life. I was being an ordinary girl, instead of overthinking life and watching my back, literally.

One day, I was leaving school for home, headed to the bus stop when this guy in a jeep pulled up to me and said, "Hey, sexy, my name is Patrick. What's your name? Do you want a ride? I quickly replied, "Hell no!" and kept walking. He then pulled his jeep over and decided to walk with me, which I found weird, but he was kind of cute. We sat on the bus stop bench and talked for a bit. He whispered sweet nothings into my ears and talked a lot about what he was doing and how he liked my legs, which I found flattering. From our conversation, I learned that he lived not too far from me. Eventually, he won me over and I accepted his invitation to drive me home. From that day forward, Patrick would pick me up after school or when practice ended, where we would get something to eat, and hang out at the park or the mall.

I enjoyed hanging out with Patrick. He was a badass, a free spirit who had dropped out of school, hung around, and sold drugs. He was not the type to keep his opinion inside. He told it like it was, and if anyone disagreed with his views, he did not care, which I found empowering. I loved that he did not give a damn about anything. I also loved that he was always available.

He quickly became everything to me. Patrick had big dreams which included me. He talked about what he wanted to do with his life after he had saved up enough money. I mostly listened as he smoked weed which I never cared for, but I was around him and the smell was fine with me. I was always afraid of drugs because of what they did to people. I feared becoming an addict.

He respected my views, which translated to me that he cared. We did everything together. It was Patrick and me against the world.

Once Patrick got his apartment, I left my sister's house and moved in with him. I was sixteen, still in school, and living my life. No one could tell me what to do. We were living by our own rules! He would smoke weed all day and go out at night. My sister was upset, but I did not care. Patrick loved me and that was all that mattered.

When my sister found out where I was, she came and took me away, sending me to live with my mother in North Lauderdale. Now I would be almost forty miles away from Miami. I was in the twelfth grade with only three months left before graduation. I wanted to remain at my school with my friends. Once again, forced to live with my mother, I felt betrayed. I appreciated my mom for all she did to care for us, but I struggled to understand her. I loved her and always wanted to show her respect, so I never talked back or even gave my opinion. I had always felt my opinion never mattered.

I finally gave in and decided to move to North Lauderdale. It was a heart-wrenching decision because I had to leave Patrick behind. He was so much fun and made me feel special. He was the first guy that truly understood me. We communicated for a while via phone calls. Sometimes he would drive up to see me or I would skip school and take the bus to see him in Miami.

I went from a predominantly black school in Miami to a school with maybe a three percent black population. I did not know anyone and became extremely depressed about everything.

Months into our relationship, Patrick got arrested and quickly moved to New York to live with his father. I was so lost because

I could not see him anymore. It took me a long time to get over him. I felt a void and was at a loss about how to deal with another disappointing abandoned relationship. I reverted to what was familiar to me. One night, I went to a party with a few of my cousins and met a handsome older guy. His name was Robert and he lived in Miami. We started seeing each other. Robert made time for me and was always available, just like Patrick. He would take me out with his friends every weekend. I would tell my mom that I was going to Miami to spend time with my sister and would stay at his apartment.

Despite all the changes in my life, I graduated from my new high school where I knew maybe ten people in my class.

"Our body has a warning signal of health issues we often overlook until it's too late. Pay attention to the whispers."

CHAPTER 4

UP AGAINST THE WORLD

After graduating high school, I immediately got a job as a sorter at a microfiche plant. Six months into the job, I had saved up enough money to move out of my mom's house and into an apartment with a friend, Goody. She was in nursing school and working. We both struggled financially. In a sense, we needed each other.

I was still dating Robert, but I became bored with our relationship. He was not assertive, just too laid back and I did not like that. I wanted a man to take charge. We continued to date although I would begin going out with other men. My trips to Miami became fewer as our relationship was no longer my priority. He wanted to spend more time with me, but I always made excuses. I was no longer dependent on him to give me money or take care of my needs. I was focusing on myself and building a better life. I worked more hours and got a second job at night to save up more money. I was being proactive about planning out my life.

One of my most incredible memories was when I went to the car dealership where my sister worked to purchase my first car. I saved up three thousand dollars in one year. I got a driver's license, but I honestly could not drive. I was nervous and probably hit every one of those light indicators on the road. My baby was a red two-door Chevy Cavalier. Life was great and with a car, I felt empowered.

Yes, I was Miss Independent. I was dating and clubbing with girlfriends and had the time of my life. The men I dated were not doing much with their lives or they were trying to escape their broken relationships. In the back of my mind, I craved a sense of security, but deep down, I knew it did not exist. Security was just another illusion. I played along for years. I got comfortable with relationships to fill those voids that were missing. I felt used and discarded and in return, I became a master of using men to my advantage, or so I thought. But I was the one getting played in the end. This vicious cycle continued for years.

I found comfort in working and earning my own money. It was at work at a new job when I met Ivan. At first, I was not interested because I did not want anything or anyone distracting me from my work. But I was flattered by all the attention he was showing me. Before I bought my car, he would pick me up and drive me to work, buy me lunch, and even drive me back home after work.

After months of his relentless pursuit, I gave in. Ivan and I had a superficial relationship in the beginning which was okay with me. He had a wife at home and was just doing his thing. I also did what I wanted to do. I was still dating other men, including visits to Robert from time to time.

Ivan and I remained in a relationship for a year until it got real. I fell head over heels in love with him. I wanted more, but he was not always available physically.

As time went on, I felt like I could not escape the patterns of my past. My heart was wired wrong because I was permanently attached to unavailable people. I finally left Robert for good. I was in love with Ivan and knew that he was the one. I knew that the first man who made me feel secure would be my husband. Unfortunately, Ivan was taken, but that did not stop me from pursuing a more meaningful relationship with him. About ten months into our relationship, I found out that I was pregnant. I was scared out of my mind. Deep down I thought that he would probably be more present if I had his child. There was absolutely no hesitation on my part. That sealed the deal.

I believed in a fantasy, that once the baby was born, Ivan would finally make up his mind, leave his wife, and be with me forever. He would step up to take care of us and he would completely devote himself to our family. Ivan was going to be my husband no matter what. I could not accept the idea of another man being in my child's life. He did not verbalize his opinion when I announced my pregnancy. He was quiet. He just listened as I offered clues about what I wanted to do.

A few weeks into the pregnancy, our relationship became very unstable. This was just as I started looking for an apartment and made changes to adjust my lifestyle to be with him and the baby. In my mind, we were already a family. I was very emotional and wanted to see him more. There were many nights that I did not want to be alone, which before had not been much of an issue for me. But Ivan was not there for me and the relationship became strained.

Ivan was working double shifts and taking on more hours at his side jobs which partially explains why I did not see him as much. When I did see him, it was not the same. I became frustrated and the seeds of doubt and anger began to seep in. We never really argued about anything, but now it was different. Every issue seemed to boil over. I was so disappointed with him, so I called it quits. And, yet again, I reverted to my old ways and sorted out distractions with other men and still seeing Ivan at the same time.

Months later, I deliberately got pregnant by Ivan because I wanted him to commit to me. I went to my first prenatal appointment with a mix of fear and excitement. And then my world was shattered. The doctor told me that I had an ectopic pregnancy, which happens when a fertilized egg plants itself outside of the uterus—a life-threatening scenario for the baby. My baby had to be removed as soon as possible. I was shocked and did not know how to react to the news. I just looked up and cried because the fantasy life I tried to build was all the way gone. I sat on that cold operating table as the doctor performed the procedure. I was all alone with no one to turn to or even to hold my hand. There was no hope of a future with Ivan. I had to face the reality that it was me against the world, and there was no happy ending to my story.

I left the hospital crushed. I felt dazed, lost, and abandoned. God must have been punishing me for the life that I was living. I hated myself because it was all my fault. I vowed to get pregnant again. In my small world view, that would make everything alright.

I fell into a deep depression. Once again, I shut myself off from the world and my feelings because it hurt to feel. I had no desire to go out or do anything. Work became a distraction from my situation. I severed ties with most of my relationships during that time. Ivan and I still talked, but I did not want him to see how emotional I was. In my time of grieving, I thought he would take advantage of my vulnerability. He would call to check on me, however, although I never shared how I felt after losing our child. It was painful to even think about the loss let alone talk about it.

I eventually let Ivan back into my life. I felt as if he pitied me because he would bring food for me without asking. Sometimes I would come home to a brown takeout bag on my table. It seemed like he genuinely cared. He was the constant in my life which was reassuring even as I continued to guard my emotions. I loved Ivan. We would never talk about his marriage and family. We just lived in the moment. There was nothing I could do to make our relationship as real as the fantasy in my head. Instead of being consumed by the disappointment, I took what I needed from the relationship and suppressed everything else.

"I faced the unknown, my heart filled with fear as my condition worsened, I felt that the end was drawing near."

CHAPTER 5
A WARNING SIGNAL

Months passed and I was pregnant again. Excited about another chance at motherhood. I found out that I was having a girl, a baby girl, and she was all mine. God had granted me a redo. I locked on to the hope that my baby girl would bring joy to my life. She would fill the void inside. She was the piece of the puzzle that I needed in my life to feel complete.

Two months into the pregnancy, I became very emotional about the state of my life. My mother was completely disappointed in me, and I felt like a failure. Ivan did not change at all, so I left him again. He was so comfortable with our relationship. I knew deep down that he would not be there for me. But I still loved him and held on to the fantasy. I needed to just let him go. As much as I tried to sever ties, my love for him always brought me back.

I started dating other guys while I was pregnant. One day, my car stalled while I was at the grocery store. This nice-looking, tall older guy came over and asked me if I needed help. I told him that I called AAA and that I should be okay. He smiled at me and told me that he was a mechanic. I asked myself what it could hurt. He asked me to open my hood, and the car started in a few minutes. He said, "By the way, my name is John. You have such a beautiful smile. Can I get your number?" I was hesitant, but I thought to myself that it could not hurt. We started a friendship where he would call and check on me. I would tell him about my frustrations with Ivan, and he was there to hear me out. Our relationship developed into a perfect friendship. He wanted to help me destress and we found a common interest. John was very caring and supportive. He would always cook for me, which I appreciated. He would also take me to my doctor's appointments, make sure that I had food to eat, and check on me constantly.

I started to have complications with my pregnancy. The most concerning issue was that my blood pressure was out of control. My doctor ordered me to only do light duty because of previous complications of hypertension and ectopic pregnancy, which meant I was high risk.

December 12, 1994, was a day I will never forget. I woke up with a slight stomachache. I rolled over, started to make my bed, and noticed blood on my sheets. I quickly went to the bathroom and sat on the toilet bowl to pee. After I got up to wipe myself, I noticed some blood in the toilet, and while standing up, I felt water trickling down my leg. I thought I was peeing on myself. This was different. I screamed out to my roommate Goody for help and she ran into the bathroom. She wrapped a blanket around me and then took me to the emergency room. On the way to the hospital, I was frantic and sobbing. I asked myself, "Why me? Why was I being punished?

The ride to the hospital seemed to take forever. I asked my roommate to call Ivan and my mother to let them know what was happening. When we finally arrived at the emergency room, Goody ran into the hallway and called for help. A nurse and an orderly came out with a wheelchair, assisting me out of the car. The pain was excruciating. It felt like I was stabbed in the stomach multiple times with knives. The first thing I heard came from the nurse's mouth, "She is having a miscarriage." It went downhill from there. They put me on a gurney and rolled me into the examination room. The ER doctor came into the room and started his examination. He ordered several tests and gave me some pain medications to relax me. I had an infection and my water bag was slightly breached. I was in active labor.

I stayed in the hospital on complete bed rest. The doctors were trying to get rid of the infection and develop my baby's lungs by giving me a massive dose of steroids. They kept me monitored and tried to delay me from going into labor because I was only seventeen weeks into my pregnancy. For my baby to have a fighting chance, the goal was to delay long enough to reach the twenty-one-week threshold.

I remained in active labor for about three weeks, which was horrible. The meds kept the pain at bay. One night the contractions would not stop. I had the nurse call Ivan and my mom to tell them to come to the hospital immediately. I needed their support. A few minutes later, they rolled me into the delivery room. Horrified, I prayed and tried to bargain with God for a successful outcome. I was so tired of disappointments. This was the change I truly needed, but I felt it slipping away.

The hospital staff rolled me into the delivery room by myself. I felt so lonely until I saw my mom and sister's faces as they entered the room. At that moment, I felt reassured. I was not alone and my family actually cared about me. I was in so much pain as the contractions continued. My mom held my hand to comfort me. My doctor told me that the plan was to have a natural birth so that my baby's lungs would secrete in the birth canal. This way her lungs would have a better chance of functioning properly. But my blood pressure created a problem. It put my life in jeopardy. So my doctor decided that he would perform a cesarean. Before they performed the procedure, a doctor gave me some meds to slow the contractions and reduce my blood pressure. Thankfully, about thirty minutes later, my blood pressure was regulated. The doctors went ahead with the original plan to have a natural birth.

I was drenched and sweaty and could barely open my eyes because everything hurt. I felt my mother's hands as I clenched tightly. I felt like she knew I was alive. She tried to comfort me, which I appreciate her for. Exhausted, all I wanted was for this to be over as tears rolled down my eyes. I felt like I was dying. As the monitors began making all kinds of noises, I just closed my eyes and prayed.

There were about six medical staffers in the room. A nurse told me to slow down my breathing and take deeper breaths. I focused on her voice because she seemed to be in control. Moments later, the doctor arrived and rechecked the monitor. The nurse told me to push as she read the fetal monitor next to me on the table. I took a deep breath and pushed my baby out. One of the nurses took a blanket, wrapped my baby inside of it, and hurriedly ran out of the room. I did not even hear the sound of a cry. I immediately felt cold and passed out. I was told later that I started hemorrhaging after giving birth.

As the hours passed, eventually I opened my eyes. My mom and sister were sitting next to me. I asked her for my baby. My mom told me my baby was fighting for her life, and that they were not allowed to see her yet. I was so afraid but hopeful. She also told me that my grandmother was home praying for me. That made me feel so much better. I asked my sister if they had seen my baby before the nurse took her out of the room. My sister said,

"The nurse ran out of the room so fast that she could not get a glimpse." I looked at her and started to cry. My understanding of the survival rate of premature babies made me believe I needed a miracle. Luckily, I was in the right hospital because Plantation General Hospital had a specialty unit for premature babies.

I named her Brittney. A day later, I was finally permitted to see my baby. She had survived the night. Thank God. As the nurse assistant rolled into the hospital's neonatal section, a nurse greeted me and told me that I needed to wash my hands and wear a mask. She explained what to expect because of my baby's condition. She said, "You're going into a room with very sick babies, and we are going to pass all of them to get into the ICU warm room where your baby is being cared for. There is only your baby currently in there, do not get too emotional because she will hear you. It's best to talk or sing to her because she knows your voice, which will bring her comfort." She looked at me and asked me, "Are you ready?"

I took a deep breath and said, "Yes." The nurse then rolled me into the room where I saw Brittney for the first time. She was in a little bed with a hot lamp over her. I was shocked to see how tiny she was. She could almost fit in the palm of my hand. Her body was completely covered with plastic wrap. Her mouth had an apparatus for her to breathe, a tube, and a needle in her neck. The tears fell down my cheeks as I watched her. I saw the reality of what we faced or were up against. As soon as the nurse left the room, I cried quietly so the baby could not hear me. I could not hold it in any longer. I wanted to touch her so she could feel my love, but instead, I sang, talked, and prayed to her.

Four days later, I was released from the hospital, but Brittney had an extended stay. Those four months were the longest months of my life. I returned to my life of working and would visit my precious baby daily. She was all mine, the sweet joy of my life. I put all my time into taking care of Brittney and ensured that she was cared for by the hospital staff. But I was dying inside because I wanted more. My attempt to balance work and hospital visits became increasingly difficult. My mother questioned me about spending countless hours at the hospital. One day she said, "Do you think you're wasting your time? She is not going to survive." I knew she meant well, but my mom was always complicated. I never relied on her to feel a sense of compassion or empathy. She was always a straight shooter. I could only think about my little angel who needed to feel me as she fought daily for her life. It was not the time to think about possibilities.

While I was on autopilot, my emotions were raw and, to a larger extent, debilitating. I felt the desperation of my situation. I held my baby's tiny hands while she lay in the incubator and sang to her to let her know I was there fighting with her. While I had no control over the situation, I had full control of my desire to let Brittney know that I would not abandon her. I would not allow anyone to hurt her. She was safe with me. I asked God to take my life instead. The battles were severe, and victories were overshadowed. Seconds turned into minutes, minutes turned into hours, and hours turned into days. My Brittney lived to fight another day.

It was during this time that I unexpectedly developed a closer relationship with God. I started going to church, reading the Bible, and truly praying to God to spare my child's life. For the first time in my life, I knew that God loved me and did not judge me. With Him, I could be my true self. I began to feel some peace creeping in about the person I was. God was by my side and I was not alone anymore.

During those difficult months, I continued to see John and Ivan, but all I cared about was my baby. I continued living the same life of nothingness. I was going through the motions until Ivan started coming around more often. He made sure that my bills were paid and that I was okay. He would accompany me to visits to see our daughter. We started seeing more of each other and our relationship began to grow once again. I cut off my relationship with John. Still, I loved talking to John because he did not judge me. We ultimately decided to remain friends.

As time went on, there were setbacks here and there. Some doctors had counted her out, saying that she was not going to make it. Nurses told me that I should make final arrangements and seek counseling for grief management. Despite the stream of grim prognoses and daily reports, I continued to pump my breast milk and deliver it to my daughter. Soon enough Brittney started to hit major milestones. She eventually gained strength. She was a fighter like I knew she was.

Altogether Brittney spent four and a half months in the hospital. The day that she was released was one of the happiest days of my life. I still tear up thinking about it. I was focused on one thing. I wanted Brittney to beat all the odds. I wanted her to live, but I wanted her to thrive as well.

With Ivan's help, I was able to bring Brittney home to my apartment. I was so excited. This was the best day of my life. The sky looked brighter, and the leaves looked greener. I was frightened and thrilled all at the same time. This little baby who was so fragile and needed so much care was counting on me. My family finally became what I believed I deserved, which was a wonderful feeling.

Approximately eight months after Brittney came home, I had a mini-stroke known as Bells. It was a routine day, nothing remarkable. I was at a doctor's appointment for Brittney. I went to the water fountain to get something to drink. After I poured a cup of water, something weird happened. For some reason, my mouth could not close properly or grab the cup. Water leaked out of my mouth and wet my T-shirt. I did not think much of it. But the next day when I woke up and went to brush my teeth, I started going through the motions. I looked at myself in the mirror and was shocked to see one side of my face noticeably drooped. I was scared and my heart started racing.

I rushed to the hospital where the doctors ran tests to identify the issue. That was when I received my first introduction to illnesses. I believed that the mini-stroke at the water fountain was triggered by the massive number of steroid shots when I was admitted to the hospital. The doctors told me that the steroid shots would speed up cell formation so that when Brittney was born, she would have the best chance of survival.

For several weeks after my mini-stroke, there was a side effect. My face lacked symmetry and my smile became extremely crooked. Even today, I still carry the lingering effects, but they are only noticeable when I smile. As much as I wanted to put that episode behind me, my smile is always there to remind me. I was self-conscious about everything. Once again, I closed myself off and went on with my life.

CHAPTER 6

MASKING THE PAIN

Ivan and I moved in together a few years later. My life was finally complete. Everything was great. I got my man. My daughter got the father that she needed. I thanked God for it all. Gratitude permeated my soul.

I made a covenant with God. If He let Brittney live, I was going to raise her to be a great woman of God. I was not going back on that promise. After I started going to church, I realized that I wanted to dedicate my life to God. My lifestyle was not aligned with the life that Jesus Christ wanted for his children, so I made adjustments.

On paper, Ivan was technically still married but truthfully, his marriage ended years before I came into the picture. As a Christian, I knew it was wrong for me to live with a man out of wedlock. And I grew tired of shacking up. The only thing that was missing was a marriage. We were already a family, but I knew that in God's eyes, our situation was not right. One day I came home from work frustrated because we had several conversations about him getting a divorce to no avail. Ivan made excuses and offered rationale after rationale. He felt that our relationship was fine as it was. I became increasingly angry and was ready to give him an ultimatum, so one day it all came to boiling point because I had had enough.

I was home from work and started making dinner. As soon as Ivan arrived, he took his shower and sat down. That's when I blurted out, "If you don't marry me, I'm going to leave. I am giving you thirty days." He looked at me with a blind stare and started eating. He proceeded to deflect, taking the conversation completely off track. I became enraged. Ivan knew my intentions because I went to the courthouse months before to file his divorce paperwork.

Ivan and I did not argue about my ultimatum. For some reason, he was not convinced that I would go through with leaving him. Even after thirty days, when I put Brittney's and my belongings in the hall, he was still in denial. When Ivan went to work one morning, me and Brittney moved in with my mom. Ivan was furious with me. I truly loved him, but I was not going to compromise my belief. There was no turning back. Deep down, I hoped he would come around and be with us as a complete family.

I came to the reality that no other man would be in Brittney's life. It was important for me to protect her at all costs. My past life was not going to be her fate.

Eventually, I started to see Ivan again and he began attending church with us. This was what I had prayed for. A few months into my stalemate, he proposed to me. It was far from a fairytale proposal that every little girl dreams of. His exact words were, "Okay! I'll marry you then." That was good enough for me. A month later, with a budget of $500, we got married in my mother's backyard in front of a few friends and family. I was now someone's wife and a mother with my very own family.

My life was filled with love and joy. I enjoyed taking care of Ivan's and Brittney's needs. A year later, we saved enough money to buy our own home. Ivan had always been such a great provider. He worked many hours to take care of us and I did the same. I was happy but deep down there were some underlying issues from my past that still lingered. Fear still crippled me and made me paranoid of people's motives as I grappled with the last twelve years of my life.

Ivan did not want any more children. He had a few kids from prior relationships. But I wanted a son. So I put a plan into action of deliberately trying to conceive. A few months later I got pregnant! I found out that it was a boy. I was excited. It seemed as if everything I asked God for, he was giving to me. The pregnancy went along without any major complications. I was, however, diagnosed with gestational diabetes. I had to learn about the disease and take daily insulin injections to control my A1C and hormone levels. I did everything the doctor advised because I wanted my baby to be born healthy. And although I wanted a natural childbirth, the doctor strongly recommended I have a cesarean section, which I agreed to. Otherwise, the birth was successful and I delivered the baby boy I always wanted.

My life was falling into place. I had the family that I wanted. I took a lot of time off and did not work during my pregnancy. My boss was unhappy with this situation and fired me. Still, it felt good to be a stay-at-home mom for the first four years of my son's life. I also enrolled in college before deciding to seek full-time employment.

Years later, my life consisted of working long hours and running home to prepare meals. I was Superwoman and I wore that "S" on my chest boldly. I was everything to everyone—a wife, mother, doctor, chauffeur, and counselor. You name it, I took on those responsibilities. I needed my mind and body to be occupied to avoid spending time in the quietness of my soul. I did not want to feel. I was missing that no inner joy, although my husband and children kept me anchored. My past tormented me and made me uneasy about truly expressing myself. I took everything as a personal attack. I rejected any attempt at authentic healing. A prisoner of my past, I felt powerless, ashamed, and unworthy.

CHAPTER 7

THE UNKNOWN

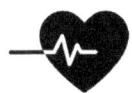

On February 28, 2014, my life was forever changed. I remember that morning as if it were yesterday. It will always be etched in my brain. I probably got about three hours of sleep the night before due to deadlines and the demands of work and school. Rarely could I get a good night's rest. While I loved my family dearly and felt quite capable of accomplishing the things that I needed to do, sometimes I felt like a hamster on a wheel, and something was making it go fast and furious.

I had a typical start to my day. At 5:00 a.m., I began my normal routine of making breakfast, prepping dinner, and getting the kids out of bed and off to school. Then I got into my car and drove to work. My thirty-minute commute to work was everything to me. It was my time to escape. I would normally crank up the music and lose myself in song, shutting out the world and the noise of traffic. But this morning was completely different. I had a major headache and kept my radio off, although the noise of the traffic did not help matters. I got to work and started planning my day while viewing emails. As a busy mother, employee, and student, multi-tasking became a necessity, a skill I honed day after day. I had been suffering for days with a headache, which I masked with aspirin. I was being a "trooper," getting things done.

I reached into my large purse to grab an aspirin, as I had done many times before, only to discover I left the bottle at home on the kitchen counter. I felt hopeless and angry, which only exacerbated my headache. I asked my coworker if she had anything that would help ease my pain. She told me that she had a prescription-strength ibuprofen. I refused her pill because it would have slowed me down and I had no time for that. Yes, even in pain I refused. I wanted to go to the store to buy a bottle of aspirin, but I did not have the time. There were too many things to do. So I pressed on.

My headache got so bad that at one point it hurt to even open my eyes. My head felt huge and heavy. My neck was struggling to support my head. My coworker Janet came over and started telling me her latest baby daddy drama, which was a never-ending story. It gave me a little time to escape. Janet was asking my opinion on her finding out about some other woman, which was evidence that her man was cheating on her. I said, "Girl, this headache is extra today." We conversed for a bit, but the conversation did not make any sense. Even her stories could not distract me from the growing pain that made my head feel like a pulsating bomb ready to explode. At one point she told me, "Girl, something going on. You need to call your doctor because you're not making any sense." Janet was right, something was off. I could not even concentrate so I told my boss I was not feeling well and decided to go home. I needed a few hours of rest before school later that evening; I had a test to take. I was certain that a nap would reset my body and I would be ready for my test later.

As I drove home, I could not fully open my eyes. The light outside was extremely bright for some odd reason, and it affected my sight. Everything appeared blurry. I was in excruciating pain. Only God knows how I made it home.

I grabbed two aspirins as quickly as possible and rolled myself into the bed. I was certain it would do the trick. I woke up a few hours later to my daughter's voice as she was arriving home from school. I had been sleeping for three hours. I jumped out of bed and went straight to the kitchen to finish dinner. It was almost 4:00 pm. The class would start at 6:30 pm that night. I had no time because time was always against me. As I meal prepped, I asked my daughter questions about her day at school. Yes, I was always good at multitasking.

Brittney was a senior in high school with only three months until graduation. I was both worried and excited for her as she was making her college plans. My little girl was growing up way too fast. It seemed like only yesterday when she was fighting for her life as a preemie baby.

I asked her about her upcoming math test, which I knew would be a challenge for her. In the middle of our conversation, she stopped me and said, "Mom! Are you okay?" I told her, "Of course I am, I just have a slight headache." Then she noticed that I was struggling for words. She said, "Mom you sound funny." I paid her no attention and went on with cooking. At this point, she also noticed that my walking was off as I went to the refrigerator. She said, "Mom, what's wrong with your leg? Did you hurt it?" I replied, "I'm tired."

Brittney immediately phoned my big sister Judy and told her what she observed. My sister then told her to call 911. She called immediately. I was bothered because there was still so much that needed to be done that evening. I had to finish dinner, pick up my son, get him ready for soccer practice, and go to school myself. A 911 call for a headache and some odd observations was not a part of my plans.

I got upset when the EMS came into my home with their commotion and wheeling in their stretcher, but I agreed to let them check me out. I sat down and all three of the EMS crew started working on me. One paramedic asked, "What's your name? What's today's date? Where are you? Does anything hurt?" He asked me a lot of silly questions, which I did not have a problem answering. I answered to the best of my knowledge. I was just slow to reply.

They first checked my vitals and advised me that my blood pressure at 195/100 was very high and that I needed to go to the hospital ASAP. I got angry and frustrated with the entire situation. I refused to go convincing myself that I had no time. My family's needs came first. If I was not able to care for them, who would? Besides, I had an important test to take at school. These were the excuses I ran off in my head convincing myself not to go to the hospital.

When Ivan came home, I was still in the kitchen cooking. He noticed something was off with my speech. Brittney eagerly told him what had taken place earlier and how I refused to go to the hospital. He convinced, or should I say, commanded me to get myself ready because we were going to the emergency room. As I walked into the emergency room, Ivan told the intake nurse what was happening to me. I was upset at him and wanted to go home.

The nurse then rushed out of the room. A few minutes later it seemed like everyone stopped what they were doing and ran into my room. I was afraid at that point, but still not overly worried. All I could think about was my son was missing his soccer practice, dinner not being ready, and a test I needed to take for school. How was I going to catch up and not let my lapse in schedule get the best of me? Unconvinced of this emergency, not once did I think about myself. I never lived in the moment because there was always something around the corner to deal with. I was experiencing something that I could not explain. I felt trapped, imprisoned, and helpless.

My condition went from bad to worse in a matter of seconds. I lost all feeling on the left side of my body. My arms and feet felt heavy. I wanted to move them, but I could not. It felt strange and unreal. I started to cry uncontrollably. The triage nurse called a code blue over the intercom. For a brief moment, I wondered which poor soul was in trouble. Shortly afterward it became clear that I was the code blue. The doctor and a few staff members rushed into the room and rapidly connected me to some medical equipment, started an IV, and drew all kinds of blood work. They rushed me into the CT lab to do more testing and they administered what seemed like endless shots. I could not keep track of what was happening. Everything felt like a blur.

A team of doctors came in to assess my situation. I was afraid and confused. Still, I could not move my body. My brain seemed unable to process information, and everything felt slower. My limbs were not responding. The doctor could not explain what was going on because I had the symptoms of a stroke, but the CT scan showed no signs of bleeding. His best guess was a Transient Ischemic Attack (TIA), which is like a mini-stroke caused by a slow bleed when a blood vessel ruptures in the brain. He told me that a TIA would go away on its own and I should be better in a few days.

But there was nothing mini about what was going on in my body. No, this was a major problem on all levels. Oh God! I cried nonstop. My family came and that made the situation worse because I felt like I had disappeared or had an out-of-body experience. I could see what was going on, but I could not move or talk in complete sentences. My body was not responding to my pleas to move. It felt like I was watching a movie on TV about a woman, only this time it was 100% real, 100% painful, and 100% frustrating. The nurse gave me medication that took care of the headache and calmed me down a bit.

Two days later, the doctor urged me to follow up with a neurologist as I was getting ready to be discharged by the nursing staff. Then my sister Judy arrived. She had gotten wind of what happened to me and drove up from Miami to the hospital within minutes. She demanded to talk to the doctor. She raised holy hell in that hospital, telling the medical staff that they were not going to discharge me. She told them point blank that they were going to run more tests or have another doctor see me for a second opinion because I was not going to leave until they fixed the problem. Judy said, "Don't let me make a phone call to my daughter who is a lawyer." You could see the fear and concern in the eyes of the staff. They had no idea who they were dealing with, but they quickly found out.

They took Judy's advice and performed another CT scan. This time the results were different. They found a bleed on the left side of my brain. I was officially diagnosed with a TIA.

Later, I was transferred to a hospital that specialized in stroke for further treatment. I will never forget my first day of rehab. It was terrifying. I was transported via ambulance on a stretcher and rolled down a long hallway toward a back room. It looked like the point of no return. I was still crying uncontrollably. My idea of a stroke victim was an elderly person. And here I was, the youngest person in the stroke rehab, unable to move the left side of my body. I had so many questions.

The rehab facility was so cold. My room was the last one at the end of the hallway. When my family visited, I projected a strong front for them but inside I was dying. I could not perform basic self-care needs for myself. I had never been like this before.

Then I was transferred to another rehab facility which I disliked, but endured and received my therapy there. I struggled to comprehend my new reality. It made me cry to get around in a wheelchair, which I despised. I had to do physical, speech, and occupational therapy. I wanted my old normal back. I wanted my life to go back to the way it was before.

For three weeks, I stayed at the second rehab facility and put in the work. Then I was released and would have someone assisting me at home. I was a very independent and controlling person who took pride in doing and accomplishing everything for me. So it was a very humbling experience to have someone taking care of my basic needs, the stuff that we all take for granted. I could not even go to the bathroom by myself. My husband and daughter helped me when my nurse was not there. This is not the way it should have been. I was supposed to be taking care of them. I came home and tried to pick up the pieces but it was extremely challenging. My world became quiet. I felt trapped with no escape. I spent two months learning to walk, talk, and do fundamental stuff that we all take for granted. Still, I was grateful to be alive because I had my husband and my family surrounding me with love and compassion.

"My life felt like a nightmare from which I could not escape."

CHAPTER 8

LOSS OF IDENTITY

I was broken! Here I was, a forty-one-year-old woman trapped in a body that I could not control. I found myself thinking about ending my life. I was grieving over the loss of my identity, which is a sign of major depression. I became angry and bitter. I could not see my way out of the darkness.

My family and a few friends kept saying that things were going to get better. The more they visited the more depressed I became. I was upset with God and questioned him relentlessly, bargained, and even begged for the life I once had. Why me? Why me? Oh God, I was not a bad person.

I could not look at life in the same way. All I saw was my inability to perform basic functions for myself as a woman and mother. That was way too much for me to handle. I was completely out of my element and lost complete control of my life.

As the weeks wore on, it became difficult to fall asleep for fear of not waking up. The days were long, but the nights were longer. I completely gave up on life. I had no fight within me. This feeling of helplessness was suffocating me.

One early Monday morning, my cell phone rang. It was a customer service agent from my insurance company. She told me that I was cleared to have in-home physical therapy. She gave me a number to call to set up my appointments. I needed help with my balance and movement so this news was really exciting.

Two days later, I got a knock on my door. It was my new therapist, Kim. She took down the information and assessed my capabilities. I did not like her at first. She was loud. And I felt that she was hard on me. She was not helpful in the ways I thought she should be. Kim would say, "What are you going to do when I'm not here." She would strap the belt around my waist to support my movement, but she would take two steps back and tell me to walk, knowing full well that I needed support because my legs would give up in the middle of my taking a step. Repeatedly, Kim would say if you don't use it, you lose it. Really, it was less about Kim and more about my frustration. It was hard and frustrating to try to walk and balance my body. My mind wanted to do what my body and limbs could not.

Kim and I met three days a week. She was encouraging me to fight for myself. As time went on, I started to see some progress. She got so comfortable with me that she started playing music during our sessions. I felt great because it took my mind off my situation. We celebrated the first day that I was upgraded to using a cane to walk. I absolutely detested using the walker. I used to cry just looking at it in my bedroom. As I took one step down a long road to recovery, I started feeling optimistic because I was getting a small glimpse at progress. Despite it all, I learned to respect what Kim was doing during my physical therapy sessions.

While I was happy about the progress that I made, I still felt that I was failing my family. The days were long and the house was too quiet. I hated being home alone. During those times my darkest thoughts would take over. I would think of all sorts of ways to end my life.

Ivan hated going to work because he did not want me home by myself for an extended length of time. So we got a security alarm system installed, that way I could push an alert button in the event of an emergency. He also got friends and family to come over and check on me. Words cannot describe how grateful I was to have such a loving support system in my time of need.

Ivan was very attentive, but I felt worthless as a woman and as his partner because I was not living up to our bargain. We could not be intimate. I needed to be the woman he married, the woman he deserved. Ivan would come home late at night. I would hear him fumbling in the kitchen, fixing his dinner because I was not able to. He would take a quick shower and fall asleep as soon as his head hit the pillow. This went on for months. I understood the vows that we took when we got married. The vows were for better or for worse, but this was really my worst.

With all of the doctor bills, copays for hospitals, and medications, my illness had added a financial burden to our household. I had no idea how we would get by. We were living paycheck to paycheck, and everything counted. It all spiraled out of control within a matter of months. I chose not to raise issue about our financial predicament because I knew that Ivan was doing everything possible to take care of us. He had to make sure that all the bills were paid. Brittney was in her senior year in private school with about three months to go toward her graduation. Thank God that she had a part-time job, but there were still some expenses that had to be taken care of that she could not cover. I prayed to God to circumvent our income and make a way so that we could still live.

Although we were making progress and staying afloat financially, I could not see a light at the end of the tunnel. My life felt like a nightmare from which I could not escape.

CHAPTER 9

ALL OPTIONS ARE EXHAUSTED

Three weeks later, I went to bed after what seemed like a very long day. Suddenly, I woke up to a jolt of intense pain and pressure in my upper back and my shoulders. The pain was so intense that I cried out as though I were being hit with a series of lightning strikes. The pain in my shoulder was dull but the pain in my back was sharp and extremely painful. It was unbearable. Something was wrong. The only pain I could compare it to was the pain of childbirth. It was exactly like contraction pains because it came in waves, which was strange. I had major sciatica problems for years, so I had a share of pain medication on hand but knew that Oxycodone and Percocet would not fix this problem. It was that intense.

Why was this happening? Why in the middle of the night? These were only some of the questions that I asked when moments of relief came. I thought maybe this was a symptom of post-traumatic stress or depression.

My husband woke up startled. He asked me what was going on, but I had no answer. All I said was, "I'm in pain. My back, my back."

He jumped up and took me to the hospital immediately. On the drive to the hospital, trying to help he said, "You're going to be alright. It's probably a sciatic nerve acting up." I knew this was different than just my sciatica. I started taking deep breaths to try to relieve the pain. My head was spinning and I felt faint. I closed my eyes and started praying to God for help. It seemed like the hospital was in another country because it was taking so long to get there.

Finally, we pulled up to the emergency room. My husband told security to bring a bed out and call a doctor to the car. The last place on earth I wanted to be was inside a hospital again. But as fate would have it, there I was in the ER with major back and shoulder pain. I was diagnosed with sciatica two years prior in the same ER waiting room. The nurse came out with two other staff and got me on the bed, and started asking questions,

"Where does it hurt?"

"When did the pain start?"

"What did you take?"

"How bad is the pain?"

Medical staff rolled me into triage and started connecting me to machines and drawing blood. The doctors ran an EKG test. The results came back quickly showing an abnormality. I looked over to the machine and noticed the lines on the paper were erratic. The lines would go up for a bit and come down. I was concerned but still unsure about what that had to do with my back and shoulder pain.

Then I had a chest X-ray. This was followed by a CT scan and echocardiogram. More abnormalities were discovered. They gave me a series of shots to take away the pain. They seemed to be in quite a rush to get all these tests done. I wanted to know why this was happening, but the more urgent need was pain relief.

The doctor came into the room and told Ivan and me that he was going to send me to a different hospital for advanced testing. I immediately asked why. He said that they needed to study my heart with specialized testing equipment. Just what I needed, more testing! I was really concerned and terribly afraid. I said, "My heart! Is something wrong with my heart?" I saw the look on my husband's face as the doctor gave us more details. The doctor wanted to know more about my timeline and my history. Ivan looked both dumbfounded and concerned. He has always had a hard-core way of life, and he never truly expresses his feelings, but that day he was in a state of pure panic. In a matter of seconds, his poker face melted away. Now it was showing desperation and confusion as if there was a mix-up and, at any moment, they would let us know that there was a mistake.

When I look back on first being admitted to the hospital for my stroke, I do not think the doctors ran an EKG, nor did they perform an echocardiogram of my heart. I remembered the tech taking a CT scan of my head but never my chest and my heart. It seemed as if they had missed a lot because their only focus was on my brain and not checking the heart functions

A stroke, which is a brain attack, is related to a heart attack.

It's not a question of me not being grateful, but I feel that my life could have been different if the doctors intervened earlier. And then I was on strong medications, so I wondered why they were not working. Three weeks prior, I was unable to move because of the symptoms of a stroke. Now I was attached to so many cords and wires that I could not move.

I arrived at Broward General Hospital to have a cardiac catheter test done. Ivan called his sister Pam and my sister Judy to come to the hospital for additional support. They met me at the entrance of the hospital. The EMTs rushed me into the lab where doctors were waiting to have the procedure done immediately. Pam and Judy were Godsent. Judy held my hands, while Pam kept a tight grip on Ivan's. Things were happening so quickly that I could not process it all. I failed all the previous tests, so this next one was critical.

I was confident that everything was going to be fine. The staff rolled me into a cold room with steel equipment everywhere and transferred me onto a steel bed. It was so cold that I wanted to jump out immediately as my body made contact. There were four big monitors next to the bed, and all kinds of instruments lined up. Four people in sterile garments covered from head to toe were standing ready in the room. Oh, Lord! This looks serious. The anesthesiologist came into the room and walked me through the events that were going to take place. He told me that the anesthesia was not going to put me into a deep sleep and that I would only feel a bit of pressure, but I would not feel any pain. Then he gave me the shot. The doctor and her team started working. She pushed the needle in my right leg on the side of my groin area. I could see everything that was going on. I looked at the monitors unsure of what they were indicating. Still, I held out hope that everything would be okay.

During the test, my whole world started spinning. I was in disbelief. At some point, I passed out. I would learn that a special dye was put into my arteries that would show how my heart was functioning, and how blood flowed through the arteries.

I was in recovery when three doctors walked into my room. One of the doctors came close to my bedside and said, "Hello, my name is Dr. Cantaller. I am your cardiothoracic surgeon and these two gentlemen are my interns." As soon as he opened his mouth and said the word surgeon, I knew it was not good news. This was a big deal. Words poured out of his mouth, but I did not understand. I was shocked and the entire room started to spin. I glanced over at Ivan. He had the look of pure terror, an expression I'd never seen on him before. His eye was fixated on me as if he was in so much pain. He grabbed hold of my hand with a tight grip, as the tears flowed. I looked at him as if he had answers to all the questions that were in my mind.

Why is all of this happening to me?

How did I get here?

How do I fix this?

I started replaying the events in my life, trying to grab onto something. I was a controlling person and for the first time in my life, I was unsure of what was going to happen next. This situation showed me that I was clearly not in control. I could not fix this.

One of the doctors came in closer to me and said they found multiple life-threatening blockages, and that I needed an operation immediately. I needed to have open-heart bypass surgery right away because all four of my major arteries were ninety percent blocked and that was the only option to save my life! Ivan held my hand tight. The room was silent as water flowed from both of our eyes. I tried to be strong for both of us but this time I could not. This was too much to tolerate. The dam was completely broken. I could not prevent the constant stream of tears from flowing wildly on the hospital gown.

Well, I cried out to God. I felt defeated. I had no answers.

The nurse came into the room immediately and handed my husband a stack of papers for him to sign as she explained the procedure. She asked me if I had a living will. My life flashed by– my children, my family.

After the cardiac catheterization procedure, the staff transported me into recovery. I was told to lie still for four hours. My sister and other family came one by one into my room. I asked my sister to call my pastor. I just wanted to see my children at that point. My babies needed me.

Suddenly, I felt sweaty, clammy, and tightness in my chest. I started sweating profusely. My sister looked at me with a concerned look. She asked me if I was okay! When I looked up, the room started to spin. She ran and called the nurse who came in. The next thing I remember was waking up in ICU. I looked down and saw Ivan at my bedside. He asked, "Are you okay?" I was slow to answer him. I said, "I'm good." He said, "No you're not." I was not sure of the time. I asked Ivan what time it was. He told me it was five o'clock in the morning. He then told me what took place the night before. He looked worried. He said my blood pressure went extremely low, so the doctors moved me to the ICU. He held my hand gently and whispered into my ears, "I want to tell you that I love you!" With tears rolling down his face, this was a first for me, I had never seen Ivan cry like this before. I was overcome by emotions.

I closed my eyes and took a deep breath and told myself that this was all a dream. I'm going to wake up and everything is going to be alright. I could not believe that this was the way that my life would end. I was not ready, and my kids still needed me. I wanted to cry and ball out all the emotions that I was feeling, but I knew

I had to be strong for myself and my husband. He needed me at this moment too, and I had to be present for him. I held Ivan's hand firmly to assure him that we were going to be alright. He then whispered into my ears gently and said, "In a few minutes the nurses are going to come in to get you ready for surgery."

As we waited for the nurses to arrive, Ivan said, "You are my world and everything that is good in it!" We both started to cry.

Two nurses came into the room. They were mostly silent until one nurse said, "Today is going to be a good day." I looked up without a response. Ivan stepped back as the nurses did their prep. They disconnected me from some machines that were monitoring my vitals and my heart rate. Once they were done, Ivan held my hand again as the transporters pushed me down the long hallway to the operating room. This was it. I was being rolled away to the great unknown. Would I survive? Would I see my family again?

"I looked at my reflection in the mirror and saw a stranger staring back at me. I was lost in a sea of uncertainty, a shadow of who I used to be."

CHAPTER 10

THE UNVEILING

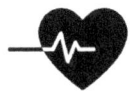

I woke up to the sound of an alarm. The room was dark and encapsulated with glass. I could hear voices in the room clearly, however I could not make out what they were saying or doing. I eventually opened my eyes and was stunned. A shiny radiant light hung above my bed. I became fixated on the light. Maybe I died on the operating table and was now having an out-of-body experience. I prayed for the angels whom I had seen in pictures to come and comfort me before taking me to heaven. A gripping and paralyzing feeling of death and fear consumed my body. Yes, I was afraid. I was very afraid.

I opened my eyes with apprehension and then looked around the room. The first thing I felt was soreness in my neck. I could not move any part of my body. Then I must have passed out again. This pattern of waking and passing out went on for days. Very frequently a nurse would run into the room and give me an injection. Although I was in a fog, at times I could hear my husband's voice and my sisters and family crying, but I could not respond. I thought about my beautiful children, and my heart ached so much because I missed them and wanted to see them. But this was not the right time. They needed to see me, but they did not need to see me suffer. If I died that would be the last image that they would have of me.

Days later, the doctors started weaning me off the pain meds, which allowed me to become more alert. I remember waking up one morning and starting to explore. I reached up to touch my neck, only to feel a bunch of tubes all around me. On the side of my neck, there was a huge needle in my carotid artery. Both arms had IV-line attachments. There was a drainage line in the middle of my lower chest, and suction cups on my feet that helped the blood to flow throughout my body. I still had minimal movement in my hands. The only thing that I had complete control over was my eyes.

The surgery was harsh. I was in excruciating pain. Imagine your chest being sawed open with a chainsaw. The chest bone is the hardest bone to crack, and to do so requires extreme force and precision. The doctors used a saw to open up my ribcage to get to my heart where they could clear the blockages. They removed a large vein from my leg and used that vein to connect a new pathway for efficient blood to my heart. They infused the bone with a titanium metal alloy mesh to close my rib cage after they fixed the issue with my heart.

I was in the intensive care unit (ICU) for two weeks under supervision, crying in pain most of the time. I remember the day the nurse removed the drainage tube that was placed deep inside my stomach. The pulling motion was intense and it felt like it went on for hours. I prayed that I would pass out to relieve the pain or at least be given some additional medications to prevent this prolonged torture.

My nurse in the Cardiac ICU was very compassionate and gentle. He made me feel safe. Anyone who has experienced nights in an ICU can understand why those nights still haunt me to this day. I could not see what was happening all around me, but

I heard everything. It seemed to go on for hours and then all the voices got eerily silent before another code blue was called, this went on all night. Again, I would hear the same commotion.

The intensive care unit felt as if it was the doorway to the other side. I was so afraid to fall asleep, unsure if I would make it through the night. At any moment I could be next to be called and that just completely horrified me. Every time the machines that were connected to me sounded off, I became frightened. I felt as if there was no escape or connection to the outside world. The small ICU room surrounded by glass windows with baby blue curtains made me feel as if there was no escape. I could not tell the day from night. But I was alive and that was a blessing.

I stayed in the ICU for six days before being moved to the telemetry cardiac care unit where I would stay to learn how to regain my strength to breathe, eat, walk, and use the bathroom on my own before discharge.

My family and friends were so supportive when I came home. Ivan was so compassionate. I felt his love throughout my entire ordeal.

Brittney was a month away from graduating high school and was preparing to go to college. I felt guilty for not being there for her like I wanted to be. I was not there to help her with her college paperwork, get ready for prom, and everything high school seniors need before they graduate. She did everything on her own.

Brittney wanted to skip her first year of college to help take care of me. I knew that would be a big mistake. I encouraged her to go without worrying about me. I did not want her to have any regrets. Although I was in pain and going through a lot of battles, I kept how I felt physically to myself. So I put on a happy face and dealt with the pain the best way I knew how.

Ivan went back to work during those initial months. He wanted to stay home to care for my daily needs, but we had major financial burdens that were looming. I was in a state of depression and could not sleep well because I felt like I would die in my sleep. I spent my days in the quietness of my sorrow while I planned my funeral and made my final arrangements. Every morning as I glanced over at my nightstand to see the countless bottles of prescribed medication, it was a constant reminder of the critical state I was in.

Days turned into months and time stood still. My heart was not stable and I was in and out of the hospital quite frequently. But one hospital stay stood out. l had just had another surgery due to reoccurring heart issues–I would have four separate stent placements due to two graph problems, all in one year. This was my twelfth stay. The room was filled with sunlight, yet it still felt so dark. I was sitting on the bed, cradling my body into a ball like a newborn baby rocking back and forth in her mother's embrace, needing to feel protected. I had to protect myself from emotional and physical pain. I felt every heartbeat as if I had just taken my first breath.

I then went into the bathroom where I caught a glance of myself in the mirror. I flashed back to a vivid memory of the first night I woke up in the ICU, where I had so many wires and machines hooked up to my body. I was horrified, confused, and frightened. Looking at the mirror, I asked myself, "Who is that person?" In that moment, life hit me like a ton of bricks, was I that little girl afraid, lost, and confused? It captured the sequence of events throughout my life, all of the inner turmoil, that had gotten me here to this cold place.

This place of torment I could not run away from. I was in so much pain, and here I was trapped in a body I could not recognize. I despised who I had become.

A dark cloud of heaviness filled the room. I was feeling completely hopeless so I reached into a box beside my bed and took out the bottle of my anxiety and sleeping pills that were prescribed to help me sleep. I swallowed a handful and dozed off, hoping that I would not wake up.

I never dealt with my past. All the pain and disappointments from my childhood were never addressed and I guarded my heart because of it. To this day, I cannot remember most of the horrific events that took place during my childhood. Those suppressed emotions led me to a life of isolation from others, which made me feel horrified when I was being touched by other people. That little abused girl who never knew how to trust hid deep inside of me and locked herself off from everything. That sense of not wanting to feel the human touch was so hard to accept that I would find myself crying from suppressing my feelings. Truly, I was not happy. My emotional pain manifested itself into a stroke and a heart attack which could have ended my life.

I just went through the motions until I had no choice but to feel the physical anguish of living through open-heart surgery. But God reached into my heart via the doctors to fix my broken heart. Now I had to feel everything. The pain was so intense, but it brought me to that place that was hidden. I had to grieve, feel, forgive, and let go. It was a process.

I was forced to confront my inner child during those months recovering from open-heart surgery. Healing took place in those quiet moments. I am a better person because of it. That process gave me some clarity and, as a result, I felt more free to express myself and reciprocate love toward others by living my life with purpose and praise.

CHAPTER 11

A MOMENT OF REFLECTION

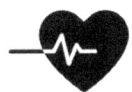

My journey with heart disease has taught me valuable lessons about living life to the fullest. Years of neglecting my health and burying emotional hurts wreaked havoc on my life over several months. I suffered a stroke and a heart attack and underwent quadruple bypass surgery. These devastating events forced me to confront issues from my past and realize I needed to make drastic changes.

I now understand that achieving wellness requires a holistic approach in all areas of life. This includes nurturing spiritual, emotional, physical, and mental health. The conscious decision to live "with passion and purpose" has empowered me to take control of my health. I strive for balance through faith, self-care, nutrition, exercise, positive thinking, and meaningful experiences. I've embraced a new mantra: "Eating to live, not living to eat."

While genetics play a role, I believe the choices I make daily have the biggest impact on my heart health. As women, we often prioritize others and ignore warning signs. I want to encourage women to make our health a top priority. Don't wait for a crisis to make changes. Start small by adding daily exercise, eating more vegetables, reducing stress, and getting preventative check-ups. Listen to your body and address issues promptly.

My journey has shown me that your attitude can impact your outcome. Despite my diagnosis, I choose to live joyfully with gratitude for each new day. There is always hope, even in desperate times. I am thankful for the doctors who physically repaired my heart, but real healing occurred when I emotionally let go of past hurts and surrendered control to God. By accepting His will and focusing on serving a higher purpose, true transformation happened.

My testimony is proof that the body can heal when your spirit, mind, and emotions are aligned. I now appreciate life's simple blessings and live fully in the present. My goal in sharing my story is to inspire other women to take control of their health, so they may live their lives to the fullest potential. Although the road is challenging at times, our inner strength can overcome it. On this journey, know you are not alone. There is always hope!

CHAPTER 12

MONITOR YOUR HEALTH

My story serves as a warning that we can no longer remain victims or pass the blame for our health outcomes to others. Never be a prisoner of your past. My heart's struggles were a lesson, not a life sentence, and for that, I am grateful.

Taking care of ourselves and staying healthy is so vitally important. It's not just about going to the doctor or eating well, but also having strong support from loved ones and finding ways to manage stress. This chapter covers everything from boosting your heart health to building resilience and feeling empowered. By focusing on these key aspects of well-being, you can truly transform your life and become a happier, healthier version of yourself. So let's learn how to thrive on our journey towards wellness together!

Just a heads up: The info I'm sharing is purely educational and shouldn't be taken as a replacement for advice from your doctor or healthcare provider. Always consult with them before starting a new diet, exercise routine, or taking any medication. It's better to be safe than sorry!

My earnest desire is for everyone to grasp the profound significance of investing in yourself by embracing self-love and dedicating the necessary effort toward personal wellness.

Monitor Your Heart Health

It's crucial to keep an eye on important indicators like blood pressure, cholesterol, and blood sugar to maintain a healthy heart. When these metrics are off the mark, it can increase your chances of developing cardiovascular disease, stroke, and other complications. But don't worry–by understanding target levels and implementing lifestyle changes and medications as needed, you can take control of your health. In this chapter, I cover conditions like hypertension and diabetes and provide actionable steps to help you keep your blood pressure, cholesterol, triglycerides, and blood glucose in check. By actively monitoring and managing these numbers, you can significantly lower your risks for heart disease and protect your heart for the long haul.

Blood Pressure Control

Blood pressure is measured by two numbers - systolic (top number) and diastolic (bottom number)

- Normal blood pressure is less than 120/80 mmHg

- High blood pressure ranges:

  o Elevated: 120-129 systolic and over 80 diastolic

  o Stage 1: 130-139 systolic or 80-89 diastolic

  o Stage 2: 140/90 or higher

  o Hypertensive Crisis: Over 180/120 mmHg is a medical emergency

- To lower blood pressure naturally:

- o Make lifestyle changes like exercising, reducing sodium, managing stress

- o Eat a balanced, heart-healthy diet

- o Stay hydrated and limit alcohol

- o Monitor blood pressure regularly

- o Talk to your doctor about medications if needed

Cholesterol Management

- Cholesterol is produced by the liver and cells to build cell membranes

- High cholesterol can cause plaque buildup in arteries, increasing the risk of heart disease and stroke

- Two main types:

  - o LDL (bad) cholesterol: Causes plaque buildup

  - o HDL (good) cholesterol: Removes excess cholesterol

- Tips to improve cholesterol levels:

  - o Limit cholesterol intake to <200mg/day if you have diabetes or heart disease

  - o Choose healthy fats like olive oil, avocados, nuts, fish

  - o Avoid trans fats from processed foods

  - o Exercise regularly, lose excess weight

- o Don't smoke

- o Talk to your doctor about medication if needed

Triglyceride Management

- Related to Cholesterol are Triglycerides which are a type of fat found in the blood that provides energy

- High triglyceride levels increase the risk of heart disease

- Triglycerides tend to increase when consuming excess calories, sugary foods, or alcohol

- There is often an inverse relationship between triglycerides and HDL (good) cholesterol

  - o As triglycerides rise, HDL tends to decrease

  - o As triglycerides decrease, HDL levels tend to increase

- Tips for lowering triglycerides:

  - o Lose excess weight

  - o Limit sugar, refined carbs, and alcohol

  - o Increase physical activity

  - o Follow a Mediterranean-style diet emphasizing vegetables, fruits, whole grains, fatty fish

  - o Take triglyceride-lowering medications if prescribed

- Keeping triglyceride levels in a healthy range can help

optimize the balance of lipids in the blood and support heart health.

Blood Sugars and Diabetes

Diabetes affects the ability to regulate blood sugar due to a lack of insulin or resistance to insulin.

- Types:
    - o Type 1: Body does not produce insulin
    - o Type 2: Body does not use insulin effectively
- Gestational: High blood sugar during pregnancy
- Symptoms include thirst, hunger, fatigue, blurred vision
- High blood sugar damages organs over time leading to complications
- Prevention and management include:
    - o Achieve/maintain healthy body weight
    - o Exercise regularly - at least 30 minutes daily
    - o Follow a balanced diet low in sugars/saturated fats
    - o Monitor blood sugar levels routinely
    - o Take medications as prescribed
    - o Limit alcohol and tobacco use

The key is making lifestyle changes like staying active, eating healthy, and not smoking to keep blood pressure, cholesterol, and blood sugar in the healthy range. Monitoring levels routinely and taking medications as needed can prevent complications from conditions like high blood pressure and diabetes.

In the Appendix, I provide samples of a blood pressure tracker and blood sugar log to help you manage your cardiovascular health and blood sugars, and use the sample medication log to keep track of your prescriptions and treatment plans.

Healthcare Support and Resources

Taking care of your well-being involves many factors, like making time for yourself and getting support from loved ones. It's also important to work with healthcare professionals, eat well, exercise, and find ways to destress. And let's not forget about the technology that can help track your progress and develop healthy habits. You combine all of these elements and you have a strong foundation of resilience and empowerment in our journey toward optimal health and wellness.

Self-Care

Self-care is so important, especially when we're sick. It's all about taking care of yourself physically, emotionally, and mentally. By managing your symptoms and reducing stress, you can improve your overall well-being and even have a better chance of recovering faster.

When you're dealing with illness, self-care becomes even more crucial because it helps you cope with all the challenges and uncertainties that come along with being unwell. It gives you a sense of control and empowers you to take charge of your health and recovery. Whether it's getting enough rest or seeking support from loved ones and healthcare professionals, self-care is essential for navigating through illness with strength and determination.

Some people might think self-care is just a luxury, but it's actually necessary for anyone dealing with illness. Making self-care a priority will both improve your overall health and help you heal faster and feel more in control. It's a powerful tool for promoting holistic well-being and facing the difficulties of illness head-on.

Family Support System

Family is so important when dealing with difficult illnesses. Their love, support, and practical help can be a lifeline for anyone facing tough circumstances. Not only do they provide emotional comfort and a sense of belonging, but they can also take some of the burden off by running errands and doing household tasks. And let's not forget how critical their role can be in advocating for the best healthcare possible. By communicating with doctors and making informed decisions, our loved ones can ensure we get the treatment we need. Having family by your side during times of illness can make all the difference in your well-being and recovery. They are there to offer unwavering love and strength during tough times, reminding you that you are not alone on this journey. So don't hesitate to embrace their support.

Health Care Team

A trusted healthcare team is essential for top-notch care and guidance on your wellness journey. Each member brings unique expertise and capabilities that can aid in managing your conditions, making informed choices about treatment, and enhancing your overall quality of life. Trust in their knowledge and be open to learning from them–it's all for your well-being!

Here are some tips to help you work effectively with your healthcare team:

- Build a good relationship with your doctors and other healthcare providers by being open and honest about your health concerns, symptoms, and treatment preferences.

- Be an active participant in your healthcare by asking questions, seeking clarification on medical advice, and advocating for yourself.

- Keep track of your medical history, including medications, treatments, and test results, and bring this information to your appointments.

- Follow your treatment plan as prescribed by your healthcare team, including taking medications as directed, attending follow-up appointments, and making lifestyle changes as recommended.

Nutrition

By incorporating more fruits and vegetables into your diet, you can have numerous health benefits, including improved digestion, weight management, and reduced risk of chronic diseases. Start by incorporating a variety of colorful fruits and vegetables into your meals, aiming for at least 5-9 servings per day. Remember to wash produce thoroughly before consuming, and consider buying organic or locally grown options when possible. Experiment with different cooking methods, such as roasting, steaming, or sautéing to find new ways to enjoy your favorite fruits and vegetables. And don't forget to stay hydrated by drinking plenty of water throughout the day. With a little time and effort, you can make healthy eating a delicious and enjoyable part of your daily routine.

Eating right gives your body the fuel and nutrients it needs to function at its best. A balanced diet full of fruits, veggies, whole grains, lean proteins, and good fats can prevent diseases, maintain a healthy weight, and boost overall health.

Here are some easy tips to start:

- Start small: Making drastic changes to your diet all at once can be overwhelming. Start by making small, manageable changes, such as adding a serving of fruits or vegetables to each meal.

- Explore new foods: Trying new fruits and vegetables can help expand your palate and make healthy eating more enjoyable. Visit a farmers market or grocery store and pick out a few items you've never tried before.

- Get creative in the kitchen: Experiment with different cooking methods and recipes to make healthy meals more exciting. Look up new recipes online or take a cooking class to learn new techniques

- Grow your own food: Gardening can be a fun and rewarding way to incorporate more fruits and vegetables into your diet. Consider starting a small garden in your backyard or on a balcony, or join a community garden in your area.

- Make it a family affair: Get your family or friends involved in meal planning and cooking. This can make healthy eating more social and enjoyable, and provide support as you work towards your health goals.

- Stay motivated: Set realistic goals for yourself and celebrate your achievements along the way. Remember that healthy eating is a journey, not a destination, and every small step you take towards better nutrition is a win.

Exercise

Exercise is crucial for our overall health and well-being for a variety of reasons. Regular physical activity can help improve cardiovascular health, strengthen muscles and bones, boost mood and mental health, and even reduce the risk of chronic diseases such as diabetes and certain types of cancer.

For beginners or those who feel intimidated to start exercising, here are some tips to help get started:

- Start slow and gradually increase intensity: It's important to ease into a new exercise routine to prevent injury and burnout. Begin with shorter, less intense workouts and gradually increase the duration and intensity as you build strength and endurance.

- Find activities you enjoy: Exercise doesn't have to be boring or feel like a chore. Try different types of physical activities such as walking, dancing, swimming, or cycling until you find something you enjoy. This will help you stay motivated and committed to your fitness routine.

- Set realistic goals: Set achievable goals for yourself,

whether it's to exercise a certain number of days per week or to improve your strength or endurance. Celebrate your progress and small victories along the way to stay motivated.

- Buddy up: Exercising with a friend or a group can make the experience more enjoyable and hold you accountable. Having a workout buddy can provide support, motivation, and encouragement to help you stay on track with your fitness goals

- Listen to your body: Pay attention to how your body feels during and after exercise. If you experience pain or discomfort, it's important to rest and seek guidance from a healthcare professional or fitness expert. Remember that rest and recovery are just as important as physical activity for overall health and wellness.

Control Stress

We often underestimate the impact stress can have on our health. It can weaken your immune system, making it easier for you to get sick. And if that's not enough, chronic stress can contribute to high blood pressure, and heart disease, and worsen existing conditions like asthma or diabetes.

But it's not just physical–stress can also mess with your mental health. It can make you feel anxious, depressed, and unable to focus or sleep properly. And let's be real, nobody likes feeling constantly on edge or exhausted all the time.

Not only that, but stress can also show up in the form of headaches, tense muscles, stomach problems, and more. It can also lead to unhealthy coping mechanisms such as overeating, substance abuse, or self-harm.

So what can you do? Well, finding healthy ways to manage and reduce stress is crucial for your well-being. Think exercise, relaxation techniques like yoga or meditation, being mindful of your thoughts, and reaching out for support from loved ones or professionals. Trust me, your mind and body will thank you.

If you're feeling overwhelmed by stress, here are some helpful tips:

- Incorporate mindfulness and deep breathing into your daily routine to calm your mind and reduce stress.

- Stay physically active by engaging in activities like walking, running, or yoga to boost your mood and release endorphins.

- Follow a balanced diet with plenty of fruits, vegetables, and whole grains to support your overall health and well-being.

- Get enough sleep each night to help recharge your body and prevent fatigue and irritability.

- Make time for activities that bring you joy and relaxation, such as reading, painting, or listening to music.

- Establish a daily routine and prioritize tasks to effectively manage your time and avoid feeling overwhelmed

- Practice effective time management techniques, such as setting boundaries, delegating tasks, and taking breaks when necessary.

- Connect with loved ones for support or seek guidance from a therapist to talk about your feelings and learn coping strategies.

- Limit exposure to negative news or social media to decrease feelings of stress and anxiety.

- Remember to prioritize self-care and take care of your mental and emotional well-being above all else.

Suggested Wearable Apps and Devices for Your Health Journey Apps

- Fitbit: A wearable device that tracks your activity levels, sleep patterns, and heart rate, and provides personalized guidance to help you reach your fitness goals.

- Food diary app: Keeping a food diary can help you track your daily intake of calories, nutrients, and water, giving you valuable insights into your eating habits and helping you make healthier choices.

- MyFitnessPal: A mobile app that helps you track your daily food intake, exercise, and weight loss progress, and provides personalized recommendations for healthy eating and exercise habits.

- Apple Watch: A smartwatch that tracks your physical activity, heart rate, and sleep patterns, and offers guided workouts and mindfulness exercises to help you stay healthy and active

- Nike Training Club: A fitness app that offers a variety of workouts, from strength training to yoga, and provides personalized recommendations based on your fitness goals and preferences.

- Strava: A running and cycling app that tracks your workouts, analyzes your performance, and connects you with a community of like-minded athletes to help you stay motivated and accountable.

- WaterMinder: A hydration tracking app that reminds you to drink water throughout the day and helps you stay properly hydrated to support your overall health and well-being.

- Headspace: A meditation app that offers guided mindfulness exercises to help reduce stress, improve focus, and promote better sleep, all of which are important for maintaining a healthy lifestyle.

- Garmin Vivosmart: A fitness tracker that monitors your physical activity, stress levels, and sleep quality, and provides personalized insights to help you optimize your health and well-being.

Devices

- Fitness tracker: A wearable device that tracks your daily activity levels, including steps taken, distance traveled, calories burned, and even sleep patterns. This can help you stay motivated and accountable for reaching your fitness goals.

- Heart rate monitor: A device that monitors your heart rate in real time, providing valuable information about your cardiovascular health and helping you optimize your workouts for maximum efficiency.

- Smartwatch: A multifunctional device that not only tracks your fitness metrics but also provides notifications, reminders, and even guided workouts to help you stay on track with your health goals.

- Blood pressure monitor: A portable device that measures your blood pressure levels, allowing you to monitor and manage your cardiovascular health more effectively.

- Smart scale: A scale that measures not only your weight but also your body fat percentage, muscle mass, and BMI can provide a more comprehensive view of your health and help you monitor your progress more effectively.

- Sleep tracker: Monitoring your sleep patterns can help you identify any issues with your sleep quality and quantity, allowing you to make adjustments to improve your overall health and well-being.

- Continuous Glucose Monitoring (CGM) systems: These devices monitor blood sugar levels throughout the day and night, providing real-time data to help users make informed decisions about their insulin dosing and diet:

  o Insulin pumps: Insulin pumps deliver a continuous dose of insulin throughout the day, eliminating the need for multiple injections. They can also be programmed to deliver additional insulin doses as needed.

  o Blood glucose meters: These devices are used to measure blood sugar levels at specific times throughout the day. They are portable and easy to use, making it convenient for users to monitor their levels on the go.

o   Smart insulin pens: These pens track the time and dosage of each insulin injection, helping users keep track of their insulin regimen and ensuring they are taking the correct doses at the right times.

o   Mobile apps: There are a variety of apps available that can help people with diabetes track their blood sugar levels, monitor their diet and exercise, and provide personalized recommendations for managing their condition.

o   Remote monitoring systems: Some monitoring devices can send real-time data to healthcare providers, allowing them to track a person's progress and make adjustments to their treatment plan as needed. This can help ensure that individuals are receiving the best possible care for their diabetes.

CHAPTER 13

REFLECTIONS OF GRACE

Scriptures of Repentance

"He heals the brokenhearted and binds up their wounds."

Psalms 147:3 NKJV

"Restore to me the joy of Your salvation, and uphold me by Your generous Spirit."

Psalms 51:12 NKJV

Both Psalms 147:3 and 51:12 helped me understand how good God is. He is the miracle worker, the promise keeper, yet why are we so afraid to forgive ourselves and seek redemption?

The concept of self-forgiveness goes deeper than simply moving on from the past. Our guilt and mistakes are too heavy to forget and move forward from easily. This is what the devil wants most of all–for us to be stuck in shame, living in fear, and feeling unworthy of Christ's love and protection. We must confront these distorted thoughts head-on, knowing that our actions have consequences. Despite the sacrifice Jesus made for our sins, we can find true forgiveness through his redeeming power and the shedding of his blood on the cross. It took me a while during my recovery to truly grasp that God can give hope to the hopeless and strength to the weak.

Scripture of Encouragement

"Fear not, for I am with you; be not dismayed, for I am your God;

I will strengthen you, I will help you, I will uphold you with my righteous right hand."

Isaiah 41:10 (ESV)

In times of trouble, it is natural to feel afraid and overwhelmed. We all face challenges in life that we may not understand; illness, job loss, and unexpected deaths are just a few examples. But God wants us to trust Him and not be consumed by fear. This message was especially meaningful to me during my own crisis, as I faced abnormal test results, missed diagnoses, emergency surgeries, and setbacks. It seemed like everything was going wrong. Yet, through it all, Isaiah 41:10 reminded me to trust in God's plan. Even when we don't understand why we are going through difficult times, these trials can strengthen our faith, teach us perseverance, develop our character and purpose, help us mentor others, and give us opportunities to share our testimonies.

Your storm will not last forever, and trials are an opportunity for your testimony of God's glory. It brings great honor to God when you have faced tough challenges but remained steadfast in your faith.

I surrendered all my fears and gave complete control to God. In return, He blessed me abundantly. The God I believe in is greater than any circumstance or adversity we may face. By releasing our worries and trusting in Him, we truly exercise our faith. As defined in the Bible, faith is "the substance of things hoped for, the evidence of things not seen." Our faith allows us to connect with God and make Him a tangible presence in our lives. While I know He can perform miracles, there may be times when we do not understand His plans for us. But sometimes, these challenges serve as lessons that strengthen our relationship with Him. Through this journey, I learned how to submit myself and trust in His plan for my life.

Dear Readers,

Thank you for taking the time to read my book. I hope that my words have inspired you and given you the courage to face whatever challenges you may be going through.

I want you to know that no matter what you are facing, God can see you through it. He is the ultimate miracle maker, and with faith and work, anything is possible. As it says in James 2:14-26, faith without works is dead. We must believe, pray, and then make the necessary effort to see our dreams come to fruition by taking care of our lives: mind, body, soul, and spirit, which means living a healthier lifestyle, making healthy eating choices, going to our doctors, removing stress from our lives, and finding community.

I pray that my book serves as a reminder of the power of faith and the importance of taking action. Trust in God's plan for you and never lose hope. Keep pushing forward, and know that you are capable of achieving great things.

Thank you again for reading my book, and I hope it has brought you some comfort and inspiration.

With love and blessings,

Hyvelle Ferguson-Davis

ACKNOWLEDGMENTS

Many people deserve to be acknowledged for their help and support during my time of need. First and foremost, I want to thank God for restoring my life when there was absolutely no way out of my situation, even when I did not understand the process or His purpose. This book is dedicated to everyone who inspired and encouraged me along my journey of healing, spiritually and physically.

To my husband, Ivan, I thank you for your unconditional love and support. I have questioned your dedication and loyalty in the past, but you have more than stepped up to be the man God called you to be. You are my soulmate, and I will forever be grateful for your love.

To my children, I love you, and I thank God for allowing me to be your guardian. You both have given me the strength and courage with a fresh perspective to live life, knowing that my legacy will remain within. You are my greatest treasures!

To my mom and siblings, I want to thank you all for being there when I needed a shoulder to cry on. I could not have ever pulled through and fought without the strength, love, and encouragement you have all given.

Thanks to my spiritual leaders, Pastor Karen and Willie Felton, at Living Word Center International church, for giving me hope. Prophetess Michelle Crump for giving me instructions that transformed my life, Pastor Paula Miller for the intervention that changed the trajectory of my life with such a divine encounter, and to all the ministers and prayer worries at Christian Life Center.

Finally, I humbly thank the medical staff and doctors at Coral Springs Hospital, North Broward, Broward Health, and West Regional Hospital, who saved my life countless times.

I appreciate you and will always be grateful to all the people that God allowed in my life. Moreover, I also stand in solidarity with those still struggling to find balance in their lives by learning to adapt despite a diagnosis.

You are my world, and I could not imagine living without your loving support.

APPENDIX

BLOOD PRESSURE TRACKER

NAME:_____   MONTH:_____

DATE	TIME	SYSTOLIC	DIASTOLIC	HEART RATE	NOTES

BLOOD SUGAR LOG

NAME: ------------------------------------- MONTH: ---------------------------

DATE	TIME	LEVEL	NOTES	DATE	TIME	LEVEL	NOTES

MEDICATION LOG

NAME:_____   DATE:_____

#	MEDICATION / SUPPLEMENT	DOSE	DIRECTIONS	NOTES
1				
2				
3				
4				
5				
6				
7				
8				
9				
10				
11				
12				
13				
14				
15				
16				
17				
18				
19				
20				

ABOUT THE AUTHOR

Hyvelle Ferguson-Davis is a passionate advocate for empowering women to take control of their heart health. As a survivor of a stroke, heart attack, and quadruple bypass surgery, she is living proof that one can thrive with purpose despite daunting diagnoses.

Driven by her journey, Hyvelle founded Heart Sistas, a 501(c)3 non-profit providing education and support for underserved women facing diabetes, heart disease, stroke, and other health challenges. Through community outreach, online resources, and workshops, Heart Sistas promotes prevention and self-care strategies focused on nutrition, fitness, and mental/emotional well-being.

Hyvelle is committed to raising awareness and closing gaps in healthcare, especially for women of color. She lends her voice to organizations like the American Heart Association, American Diabetes Association, and Mended Hearts as a board member and patient advocate.

With degrees in education and plant-based nutrition, Hyvelle is also a certified Life Coach and leadership trainer. She enjoys motivating others to make positive lifestyle changes. Her motto is "Let's prioritize our health by making health our priority, Mind, Body, Soul."

Though her health journey has been treacherous at times, Hyvelle chooses to thrive with purpose. By sharing her message of empowerment, she aims to inspire women to take control of their well-being. Because she believes that prioritizing self-care and prevention is key to combating diabetes, heart disease, and other chronic illnesses plaguing her community.

For information about

Hyvelle Ferguson-Davis,

email: **heartsistas@gmail.com**

website: **www.heartsistas.com**

Socials:

Facebook: **https://www.facebook.com/heartsistas/**

or on

Twitter: T**witter/www.twitter.com/@heart_sistas**

Instagram: **https://www.instagram.com/heartsistas/**

www.ingramcontent.com/pod-product-compliance
Lightning Source LLC
Chambersburg PA
CBHW061705120626
46550CB00003B/1095